FOLLOW THAT PAPER!
A PAPER RECYCLING
JOURNEY

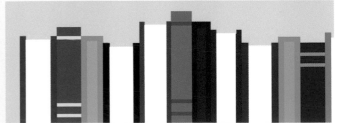

BY BRIDGET HEOS · ILLUSTRATED BY ALEX WESTGATE

AMICUS ILLUSTRATED

is published by Amicus

P.O. Box 1329, Mankato, MN 56002

www.amicuspublishing.us

Paperback edition printed by RiverStream Publishing in arrangement with Amicus.
ISBN 978-1-62243-357-5 (paperback)

LIBRARY OF CONGRESS CATALOGING-IN-PUBLICATION DATA

Names: Heos, Bridget, author. | Westgate, Alex, illustrator.

Title: Follow that paper! : a paper recycling journey / by Bridget Heos ; illustrated by Alex Westgate.

Description: Mankato, MN : Amicus, [2017] | Series: Keeping cities clean | Series: Amicus illustrated |
Audience: K to grade 3. | Includes bibliographical references and index.

Identifiers: LCCN 2015047975 | ISBN 9781607539650 (library binding) | ISBN 9781681510835 (ebook)

Subjects: LCSH: Waste paper—Recycling—Juvenile literature. | Paper industry—
Environmental aspects—Juvenile literature. | Refuse and refuse disposal—
Juvenile literature. | Recycling (Waste, etc.)—Juvenile literature.

Classification: LCC TD805 .H46 2017 | DDC 363.72/88—dc23

LC record available at http://lccn.loc.gov/2015047975

EDITOR: Rebecca Glaser

DESIGNER: Kathleen Petelinsek

PRINTED in the United States of America at
Corporate Graphics in North Mankato, Minnesota.

HC 10 9 8 7 6 5 4 3 2 1
PB 10 9 8 7 6 5 4 3 2 1

ABOUT THE AUTHOR

Bridget Heos lives in Kansas City with her husband and four children. She has written more than 80 books for children, including several about the Earth and the environment. Find out more about her at www.authorbridgetheos.com.

ABOUT THE ILLUSTRATOR

Alex Westgate is an illustrator, designer, and artist from Toronto, Ontario, Canada. He has worked for *The Washington Post*, BBC, *Reader's Digest*, and more. He drinks tap water, recycles, and throws things in the garbage every day.

When you're done with your schoolwork, you toss it in the recycling bin. Where does all that paper go? Let's follow it and find out!

The paper at school goes into a big dumpster, along with other recyclables. Each week, a front-loading recycling truck arrives at the school. The truck's mechanical arms lift up the dumpster. Whoosh! Everything falls into the truck.

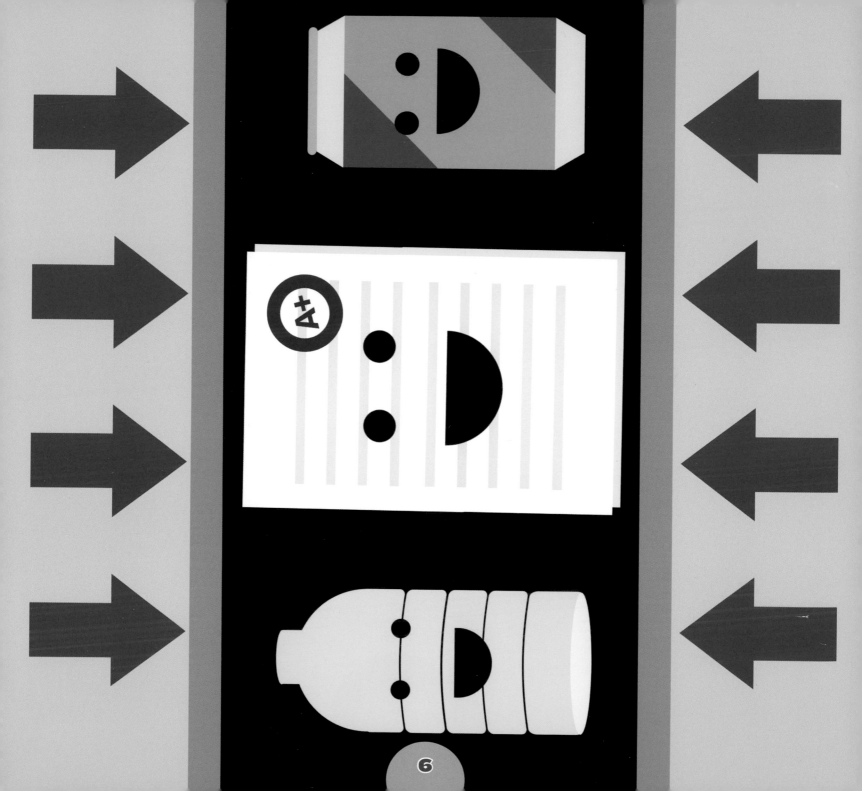

The truck visits other schools and businesses. It empties more dumpsters. In the truck, the recyclables are pressed together to make more room. That's no problem for the papers. They are already flat! Next stop, the recycling center.

All the recyclable items are dumped on the tipping floor. As they travel on conveyor belts, the items are sorted. Aluminum cans, plastic bottles, glass jars, and other items are separated. Paper is sorted too.

But not all paper is the same.
Corrugated cardboard is one type.
Newspaper is another kind.
Mail, magazines, and catalogs are
in a category called mixed paper.

Printer paper from offices or schools is called High Grade Paper. That's our paper!

Each type of paper is pressed together into a bale. The bales are tied with rope. A truck carries them to a paper mill. This is where new paper is made.

Paper is made from wood pulp, which is made from trees. When old paper is used too, fewer trees are used to make paper.

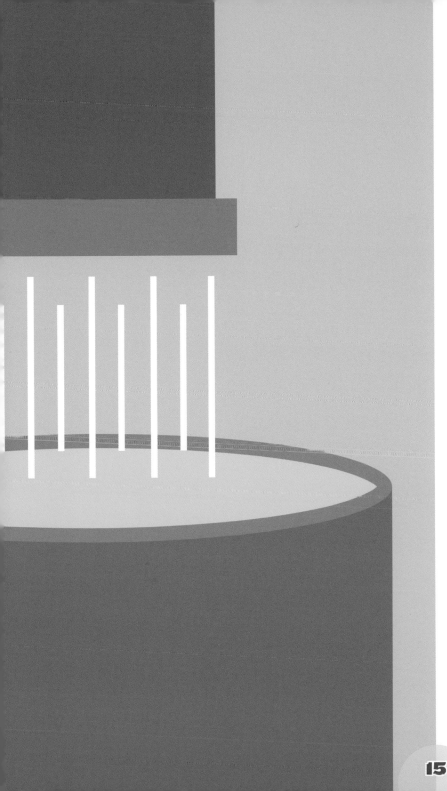

At the paper mill, the bales are broken up. The paper rides on a conveyor belt to the pulper. Hot water and chemicals are added. That turns the paper into soupy stuff called pulp.

Remember the staples from your worksheet packet? Or the dirt from the playground? The pulp goes through a series of screens to filter out dirt and unwanted bits.

"OH NO! MY A+ IS BEING WASHED AWAY!"

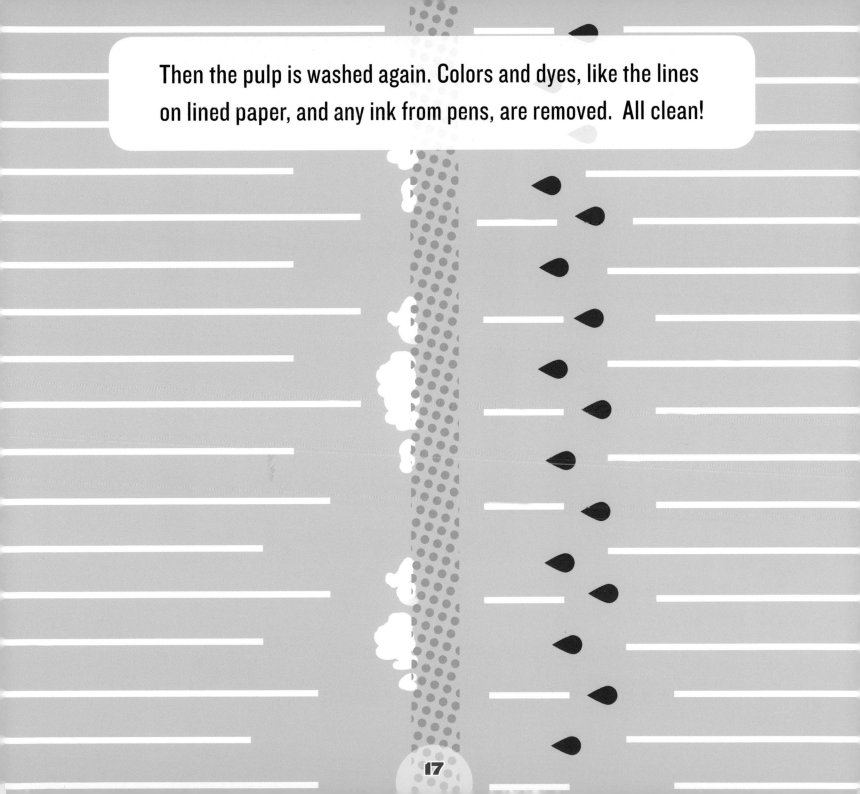

Then the pulp is washed again. Colors and dyes, like the lines on lined paper, and any ink from pens, are removed. All clean!

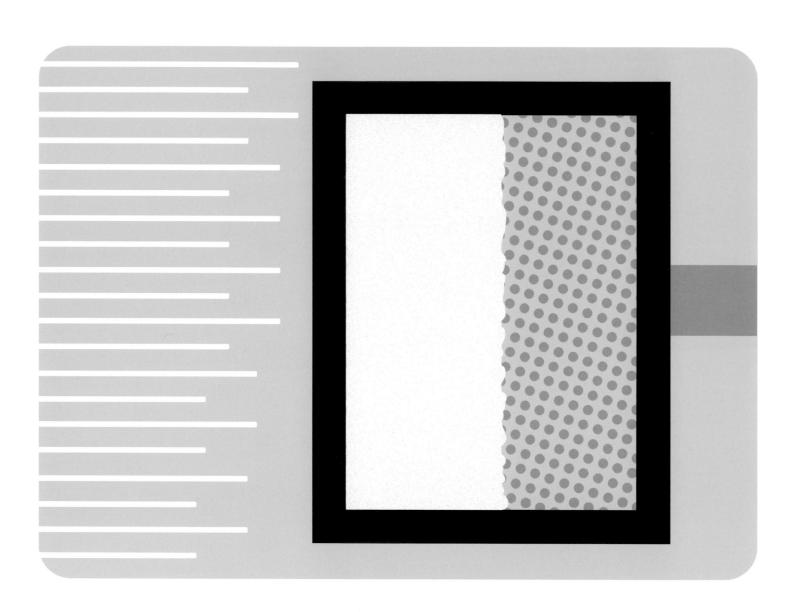

Now, a pump sprays the pulp onto a fast-moving screen. The screen speeds along at 60 miles per hour (97 km/h), and the water drips away.

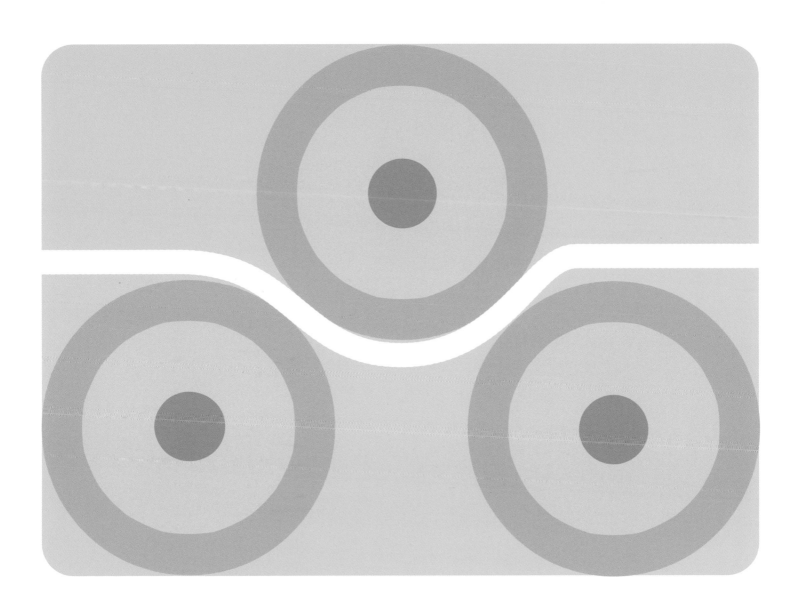

The damp paper is pressed and dried. A coating is added.
Next, it is rolled into giant rolls.

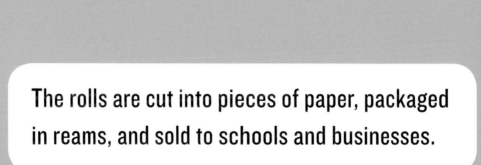

The rolls are cut into pieces of paper, packaged in reams, and sold to schools and businesses.

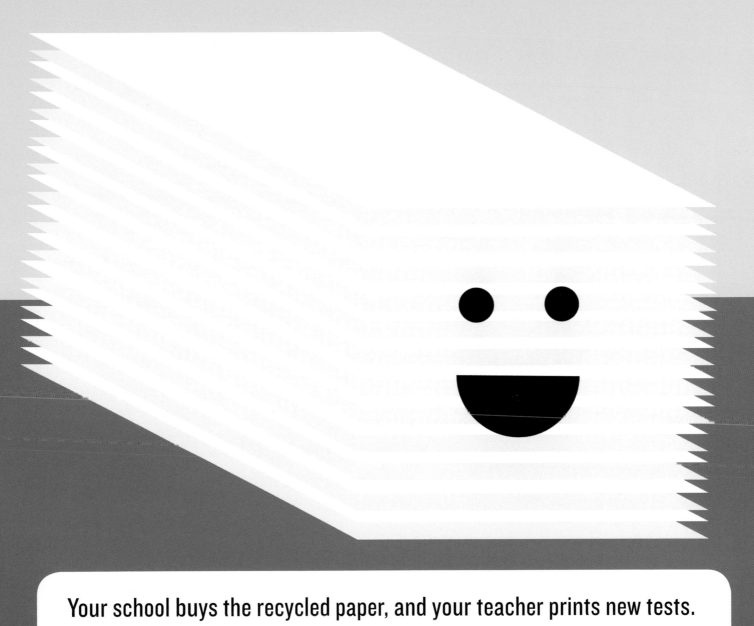

Your school buys the recycled paper, and your teacher prints new tests.
Your school gets an A+ for saving trees!

RECYCLE IT YOURSELF
MAKE PAPER BEADS

Recycle your old paper into jewelry. Be sure to ask for an adult's help!

What You Do:

1. Tear used magazines and egg cartons into 1-inch (2.5-cm) pieces. Fill up a large pot with these pieces.
2. Have a grownup pour boiling water into the pot to cover the paper and cardboard. Let it soak overnight.
3. The next day, knead the mixture by squeezing it with your hands. Then use an electric mixer to mash it up even more.
4. Press the pulp into a colander to get out extra water.
5. Shape balls around toothpicks or skewers. (These will make the hole in the bead.)
6. After an hour, squeeze out any water in the beads and make sure they are still round.
7. Let the beads dry for four days. When they are dry, you can paint them.
8. Take out the toothpicks or skewers and string the beads on yarn to make necklaces or bracelets.

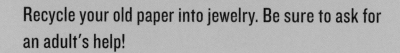

What You Need:

- [ ] Used magazines and paper egg cartons
- [ ] Large pot
- [ ] Boiling water
- [ ] Electric mixer
- [ ] Colander
- [ ] Toothpicks or wooden skewers
- [ ] Paint and brushes
- [ ] Yarn or string

GLOSSARY

bale A bundle of material pressed and tied together.

mechanical arm A metal claw or spike that lifts the recycle bin up so that it can be emptied into a truck.

paper mill A factory where paper is made.

pulp A soupy mix of fiber, water, and chemicals used to make paper.

ream A quantity of paper, often about 500 sheets in one package.

recyclable An item that can be remade into new things.

READ MORE

Fix, Alexandra. **Paper**. Reduce, Reuse, Recycle. Chicago: Heinemann Library, 2008.

Maloof, Torrey. **We Recycle**. Huntington Beach, Cali.: Teacher Created Materials, 2015.

Nelson, Robin. **How I Reduce, Reuse, and Recycle**. Minneapolis: Lerner Publications Company, 2014.

Rodabaugh, Katrina. **The Paper Playhouse: Awesome Art Projects for Kids Using Paper, Boxes, and Books**. Beverly, Mass: Quarry Books, 2015.

WEBSITES

ESchool Today Waste Management: Recycling Paper
http://www.eschooltoday.com/waste-recycling/paper-waste-recycling-process.html
Read about paper recycling.

Kids Recycling Zone
http://www.kidsrecyclingzone.com/
Discover more uses for recycled materials and learn how you can make a difference by recycling.

PBS Kids Zoom: Activities from the Show—Recycling Paper
http://pbskids.org/zoom/activities/sci/recyclingpaper.html
Learn how to make your own recycled paper.

Every effort has been made to ensure that these websites are appropriate for children. However, because of the nature of the Internet, it is impossible to guarantee that these sites will remain active indefinitely or that their contents will not be altered.